TEA
BLENDS · ORIGINS · RITUALS

Written by Rob Alcraft

TOP THAT!™

CONTENTS

3

THE STORY OF TEA

The beginning of tea is the stuff of legends. In one tale, the first tea grew from the eyelids of a Buddhist monk, Dharuma, who traveled to China in the 5th century. Unable to stay awake as he meditated, Dharuma cut off his offending eyelids, and cast them away. Where they fell a tree grew—the tea tree—which made a drink that could drive away sleep.

Another legend relates how, in 2737 BC, the Chinese emperor Shen Nung discovered tea by accident, when leaves from a tea tree fell into water being boiled to drink.

Among the first written references to tea is a 7th-century Chinese medical text. Tea is recommended as treatment for abscesses and ailments of the bladder. It was also said that tea "gladdens and cheers the heart."

THE FIRST TEAS

Sichuan, in the west of China, was probably where tea was first grown and drunk. In earliest times the fresh, unprocessed leaves of the tea plant were simply boiled in water. By the 9th century, leaves were being steamed and compressed into cakes. To make tea, these cakes (which were also used as money) were pounded up and boiled in water.

By 1300, the Chinese were infusing leaves in boiling water. This is the tea-making method they passed to European travelers and Dutch and Portuguese merchants. The traders from Amoy called the new drink "te;" those from Canton called it "chaa." The Portuguese called it "Bohea." Tea, as we know it, had arrived.

EUROPE'S FIRST TEA DRINKERS

The Dutch were the first tea drinkers outside Asia. They were the first to establish trading links with China, early in the 17th century, successfully fighting off the British.

In fact, when tea, so often thought of as the British drink, arrived in London it came via Holland and the Dutch East India Company.

Trade with China was far from straightforward. Dutch traders were originally invited to Canton to trade once every eight years, and even then only twenty men would be allowed.

Despite the difficulties, tea became popular in Holland and, by 1680, ordinary people were buying tea. The Dutch love of tea was in part down to an eminent physician, Cornelius Decker. Dubbed Dr Good Tea, he advocated drinking between 40 and 50 cups a day, more if it could be managed. Eight cups a day was claimed to be a good number for a novice tea-drinker.

Women in Holland were the customary tea buyers, buying their tea from apothecary shops where tea was sold. They would first smell samples of tea, before having them brewed in the shop so they could taste them. Often they would carry their own teapots for the purpose of brewing up samples.

Tea was also sold ready-brewed from street barrows, and at inns. At inns travelers could brew their own tea outside in the gardens, getting a complete tea service to themselves, including a kettle and stove.

Tea arrives in Britain

When tea arrived in Britain in the 1650s it was the drink of royals, courtiers, and the super-rich. The diarist Samuel Pepys, a minister in the government of Charles II, who learnt to drink tea while in exile in the Hague, records his first cup of tea on 25th September, 1660. He writes that he "did send for a Cupp of Tee (a China drink) of which I never had drunk before..."

Tea became popular, but was extremely expensive. Household accounts of 1690 show the price of tea bought by Mary, Countess of Argyll. It cost more than $43 (£26) a pound; nearly $3,300 (£2,000) at today's prices, and more than ten years' wages for a 17th-century footman.

Tea drinking spreads

Tea was first sold in coffee houses—named after coffee only because it arrived in Britain first. Forerunners of the gentlemen's club, coffee houses were places to associate and talk. From the earliest times of tea in Britain it was linked with informal gatherings and conversation.

The taste for the new drink was not confined to Europe. When the British took control of the Dutch colony, New Amsterdam (renamed New York in 1674), it was said to be consuming as much tea as its new colonial master. By the next century fashionable ladies in Boston were proudly taking their own teacup and saucer to social gatherings.

THE TRADE IN TEA

At first, tea in Britain was so expensive because of the cost of importing it.

It could take two years to bring tea from China to London. An entire season's crop could be lost to flood or disaster before the tea even left China.

The English ships, known as East Indiamen, which carried tea from the Chinese ports were large, sluggish and heavily laden. Setting sail in January with cargoes of tea, silk, spices, and porcelain, they would not arrive in London until the next winter.

THE EAST INDIA COMPANY

Tea was also expensive because one company—The East India Company (originally known as the John Company)—had a monopoly on the trade. Granted in a charter by Elizabeth I in 1600, the monopoly gave the East India Company such power that it was more empire than trader. It could declare war, negotiate peace, pass laws, and inflict punishment. Backed by British naval success it eventually controled all trade with China and India.

TEA AND FREEDOM *The Boston Tea Party*
Under British rule, the popularity of tea in America continued to grow. Smuggling helped, avoiding British duties and taxes and keeping prices down. By the mid 18th century, tea parties were a vital social occasion for fashionable ladies from Boston to New York.

But in 1773 Britain passed the Tea Act. It levied a new three pence a pound tax on tea and gave the British East India Company a monopoly on all tea sales to the American colonies. Tea was to be sold only by a few approved merchants. It looked like the end of free trade for the American colonies.

Later that same year, in October, a consignment of tea was loaded in London, bound for America. Word preceded it across the Atlantic that this tea was not only taxed, but had sat in the warehouses for months and was practically rotten. The colonists were being duped. One New York newspaper, the *Alarm*, warned, "If you touch one grain of the accursed tea you are undone. America is threatened with worse than Egyptian slavery." In Boston, destined to receive 342 chests of the tea, hundreds of women pledged to rid their houses of tea completely. By 28th November, when the first of the ships, the *Dartmouth*, arrived in Boston carrying tea from London, no one was prepared to see the tea unloaded. It was to return to London, a symbol of all that was wrong with rule from Britain.

For eighteen days there was a stand-off. The *Dartmouth* went nowhere and the tea was not moved. Then on the nineteenth day the tension broke and, in what became known as the Boston Tea Party, fifty men stormed the ship and dumped its cargo into the harbor. Over the next months, from New Jersey and South Carolina to Philadelphia, British tea ships were stormed and their cargoes dumped overboard. The tea protests helped to radicalize the American colony and crystalize anger against the British. From tea would come revolution.

TEA, TIME AND FOOD

Before the arrival of tea to drink, meal times for most well-off families were extremely alcoholic. There was ale even for breakfast, and the main meal was accompanied by large volumes of beer, liquor and wine. Diners often drank themselves under the table.

Tea began to change everything. The fashion developed for ladies to withdraw to a small closet or bedroom escaping the loud, drunken conversation and tobacco smoke. Men too, started to drink the new tea after meals, and by the 1750s breakfast in a fashionable household included tea with hot buttered toast. Not everyone approved of the new

ways, and
time call
Indian p__

But this view was in
every fashionable, wealthy ho
had its collection of delicate teapots,
cups, and accessories.

AFTERNOON TEA

During the 18th century, British
eating habits and meal times began to
change. By early Victorian times, dinner
had moved ever later, to 7:30 or 8 pm.
For the Duchess of Bedford it was too
long to wait, and around 1840 she took
to having her tea things brought to her
room for five o'clock tea. At first it was
private, then teatime took place with
friends. The idea of afternoon tea, and
the invitation to it, seemed enchanting,
and the ritual of afternoon tea was
born. It wasn't long before "afternoon
tea" had become a social institution.

TEA FOR EVERYONE

From the earliest days, tea brought people together. The wealthy, the ordinary and even the criminal visited the new tea gardens that opened in 18th-century London. Modeled on a Dutch idea of taking tea outside, people could walk and be entertained, dine, and drink tea in private summer houses.

Tea was a great leveler outside London. Servants in Britain's great houses had tasted tea, and by the mid 18th century, many servants had their wages calculated to include a tea allowance. Mill owners and landowners began to provide tea for workers as a more productive alternative to ale and spirits.

Smuggling, played an important part in bringing tea to the masses. Smuggled tea could be had for half the price of official tea. A 19th-century report—the Commission of Excise on Smuggling—estimated that nearly $1.6 million (£1 million) was lost annually in revenues on smuggled tea: an immense sum for the time.

In 1833 the East India Company monopoly was ended. Taxes on tea were successively reduced; new, cheaper teas arrived from India and Ceylon and consumption soared. Tea was now for everyone—a unique blend of necessity, pleasure, and luxury.

FROM BUSH TO CUP

Tea is grown in eighteen countries, across the tropics in Asia, to Africa and South America, from countries as different as Kenya, Sri Lanka, Argentina, and Indonesia.

CHINA

GEORGIA
BANGLADESH

TURKEY

JAPAN

IRAN

CAMEROON

INDIA

TAIWAN

KENYA

SRI LANKA

INDONESIA

UGANDA

TANZANIA

MALAWI

MOZAMBIQUE

BRAZIL

ARGENTINA

Tea plantations have even been tried in the southern states of America.

Tea is made from the young leaves and buds of the evergreen tea tree, *camellia sinensis*. In the wild, tea trees can grow to 860 feet (18 m), with delicate, scented white flowers and smooth dark brown seeds about the size of a penny.

TEA TREE

There are three varieties of tea plant, with many other hybrids recognized and cultivated by growers. The Assam variety, used mainly for black teas, has large, glossy leaves between 1.5-3in. (4-8 cm) long.

The China variety normally grows as a shrub up to 10 feet (3 m) high. It has small, matt, deep green leaves.

The Cambodian variety can grow to 32 feet (10 m) and has long, narrow, turned-up leaves that can take on a reddish tinge in the fall.

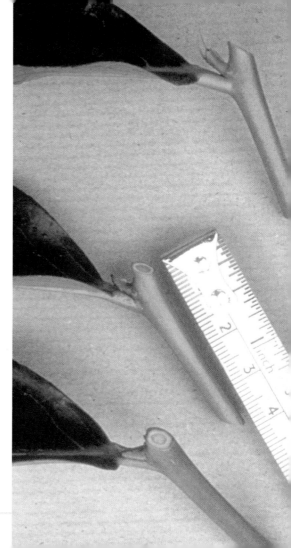

TEA GROWING

Tea begins life in a nursery as a clone. Mother bushes are selected and pruned to produce long shoots which are cut and propagated in shady beds.

One mother bush can produce a thousand clones over a year. Tea can be grown from seed, but only a cloned plant will give a known and consistent quality of tea.

The clones are planted out at a year old, in rows about three feet apart. They are cut twice a year until they are around two or three years old, when they first begin to be picked for tea. A tea bush can have a 75-year life, or longer, depending on the way it is cropped, pruned, and manured.

16

Some bushes in Sri Lanka are still producing tea over 125 years after they were first planted.

PICKING TEA

Picking tea is hard, skilled work and one of the most important parts of the tea process. The high level of skill and discernment needed means that it is almost always still done by hand. In fact, one of the main requirements of tea production is labor.

Tea is picked back to what is known as the plucking table—giving tea estates the fresh green, rolling look of neatly-trimmed hedges.

Each new growth, or flush, of tea is plucked at roughly one-to-two week intervals. Pickers, almost always women, move from bush to bush taking two leaves and a bud. Each bush takes 30-45 seconds to pluck. One picker can pick around 60–80 lbs of green leaf a day.

TEA MAKING

It takes around 100 lbs of green leaf to make around 20 lbs of finished tea.

First the picked tea is taken from the fields to tea factories, on or close to the plantation. The tea is then withered, or air-dried, in long wire-mesh troughs. Withering, which can take up to seventeen hours, reduces the moisture in the leaf by around seventy per cent, and makes the leaves soft and pliable.

After it is withered, tea is passed through mechanical rollers lined with teeth that cut, tear, and curl the leaf, reducing it to small pieces. This process begins fermentation. During fermentation tea oxidizes, turning through green to dark brown. This helps create the strength, color and flavor of finished black tea.

Temperature and time are crucial in fermentation. It can take between thirty minutes and two hours—too long or not long enough and the tea can be spoiled.

As soon as the fermentation has reached the right stage the tea is dried or fired and fermentation stops. The tea as we know it is ready to be graded and packed.

OLD METHODS

Not all tea is manufactured in the same way. Green teas are not fermented before they are fired. Some green teas are also still rolled by hand, while others are steamed.

Some black teas, especially delicately-flavored large leaf teas like Darjeeling, are still made in the old, more time-consuming way. In this method machines simply roll tea, giving such tea its characteristic twisted appearance.

GRADING TEA

All tea is sorted as it is made, and then graded. The grade describes a tea's leaf size and type. Sometimes the name of the tea reflects its grade, for examples Lapsang Souchong (souchong is a large grade whole leaf tea, rolled lengthways.) Even so, most of the time only dealers and blenders are aware of a tea's grade.

BLACK TEA GRADES

The four main grade categories of black tea are whole leaf, broken leaf, fannings, and dust with many categories in-between. Most tea found in tea bags today is graded as dust, and consists of small broken bits of

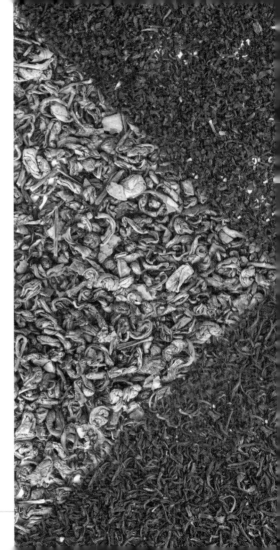

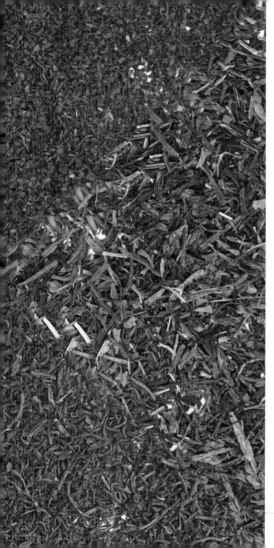

leaf, typical of teas that are cut, torn and curled, rather than rolled. Dust tea can brew strong tea quickly, making it ideal for tea bags. Whole leaf and broken leaf tea can give better flavors, and there are a large variety of whole leaf grades, the most prized having plenty of fine tips from new buds.

GREEN TEA GRADES

Green tea is graded according to the way its leaf is rolled, its size and the tea's place of origin. The main grades are Gun Powder, Young Hyson, Hyson and Imperial.

The Chinese themselves categorize green tea into five groups—red, green, yellow, red brick, and green brick. Each of these is divided into rough, tender, old and new, and then divided again according to whether the tea is well or badly made, and according to its origin. Thus there are many hundreds of grades of green tea, many made by hand, and very few of which are exported.

TEA FOR SALE

For many pioneer tea drinkers, their first experience of tea would have been a ready-made brew served in coffee shops, which generally entertained an all-male clientele. The tea wouldn't have been particularly fresh, or even pleasant, as barrels of tea served through the day would be prepared in the morning so that excise men could levy tax on them. And, given its fabulous price, tea was often adulterated or bulked out with leaves, ash, used tea, and even sheep dung.

As tea became more popular people, women in particular, wanted tea at home. Tom's Coffee House, opened in 1706 by Thomas Twining on the Strand in London, was the first coffee house where respectable women could actually go in to buy tea themselves.

THE TEA TRADE

In 1839 the Indian state of Assam's first export of tea amounted to just 340 lbs. Today the world production of tea is nearly 3 million tonnes. The largest producers are China, India, and Sri Lanka. Kenya, Taiwan, and Indonesia are also important in the world of tea production.

The world tea trade revolves around weekly auctions in Calcutta, Mombasa, Colombo, and Jakarta. Tea brokers list the teas coming to auction, and send samples to buyers. Buyers grade the teas on offer, and at the auction bid for those they want.

THE TEA PRICE

As well as being sold by auction, tea is sometimes sold by private treaty.

In this trade dealers and tea merchants buy from individual estates, basically gambling that the quality and price they can get will allow them to sell the tea on when prices rise.

FAIR TRADE TEA

Whatever the price of tea, the tea pickers and estate laborers often receive only a fraction of the price paid for a packet off the shelf.

Fair trade teas—where tea is bought direct from growers and tea workers —are a way of ensuring that a little

more of the money paid for tea by consumers gets through to those who grow, pick, and process the tea.

Concentrating on quality and local production, fair trade tea provides a better return to laborers, guaranteed prices, and profit share schemes.

TAKING TEA TO MARKET

Curiosity—and the fact that all the right people were drinking it, including King Charles II—sold the first tea.

After that competing merchants had to work harder. Many based the appeal of their tea on its blend, often creating special blends for royalty.

But the competition and marketing of tea really took off after the end of the East India Company monopoly. In 1833, for the first time, tea could be landed and traded at any port in Britain. This free trade gave rise to many household brands that we still recognize today. Lipton began trading tea from Glasgow and the familiar yellow and red packaging and brand is now famous all over the world.

CLIPPER SHIPS

The American clipper ships revolutionlized the shipping of tea; much faster than any other trading ships, the new ships could make the round trip from New York in just eight months. In the past the East India men could take fifteen months to reach Britain with the new teas from China. In the 1850s British companies began building clipper ships too, giving rise to an unplanned publicity coup. Each nation raced to have the first ships home, the cargo of the first arrivals being guaranteed to make huge profits.

The races caught the public imagination. Telegrams would report the ships' progress. Crowds would gather at the quayside to see the ships home—and tea would be tasted and sold by 9 am and on its way to stores. In one famous race between the clipper ships *Ariel* and *Taeping,* only twenty minutes separated the two ships, after 99 days of sailing.

FROM BAGS TO BIG BUSINESS

The tea bag—which first appeared in homes in the 1960s—was the biggest change to the way tea was sold.

Tea bags were initially invented by American tea merchant Thomas Sullivan who, in 1908, sent out samples of his new teas in small silk bags. He thought people would tip the tea into the pot as normal, but they didn't. They brewed the tea from the bag, and complained when their orders of tea didn't arrive packaged in the same way.

After the invention of the humble tea bag, the fortunes of tea were only to improve. As new and established companies vied for custom in an increasingly crowded market, the marketing and advertising of brands was to become an important element of the industry.

Perhaps surprisingly, one of the most successful campaigns in the US, Canada, and Britain, was the addition of small picture cards to packets of tea, which generally ran in themed series such as birds or dinosaurs.

The international company Brooke Bond, and its brand Red Rose, led the way in the marketing scheme. The height of the campaigns was reached in the 1960s and '70s, when tea cards were collected avidly by children who made sure their parents continued to drink the right brand of tea.

Coupons, offers, and free gifts were, and still are, common devices to promote sales but these days the influence of television is arguably the most powerful form of marketing tea. Some of the most successful advertisers of tea in Britain were chimps, who first appeared on television in 1956, advertising Brooke Bond's PG Tips. A well-loved TV chimp with the public was Rosie—even though her favorite drink was really gin and orange!

TEA AND HEALTH

Tea has always been associated with good health. It was first used in China exclusively as a medicinal drink. This reputation followed tea to the Netherlands, where Dr Decker endorsed its benefits, and on to Britain in the mid 17th century, where Thomas Garway would promote the virtues of tea.

Thomas Garway, the first tea seller, who sold tea from his coffee house in Exchange Alley in the City of London, wrote in a shop-bill, or advert, that "The Drink is declared to be most wholesome, preserving in perfect health till extreme Old Age." He went on to list fourteen ways that tea protected health, including: improving sight and memory, flushing away kidney stones and even curing lipitude distillations—nowadays known as the common cold.

In fact tea was, at first, anything but healthy. It was often adulterated, mixed with dung, even recycled, dyed and re-sold. Yet people still believed tea was healthy, and a few years after first tasting it himself, Samuel Pepys, recorded that his wife was being prescribed tea by her doctor.

TEETOTALISM

In the 19th century, tea was at the center of the Temperance Movement: a campaign to cut the massive consumption of alcohol that made drunkenness the normal state of affairs for many people, whatever the time of day.

Supporters of temperance advocated tea as an alternative drink, and the word teetotal was coined for people and events that were alcohol-free. Tea meetings and tea festivals were organized, where people would take the pledge to give up drink. By the beginning of the 20th century temperance, and fashion, meant that tea was the drink of choice for all occasions, and no party was complete without it.

CAN TEA MAKE YOU LIVE LONGER?

Current evidence about the health benefits of tea is not conclusive. But it is thought that tea, or more accurately the antioxidants it contains (also found in fruit and vegetables) may reduce the risk of heart disease, strokes, and cancer.

Certainly moderate tea drinking helps replace essential liquid that our bodies lose. The other benefits to remember are that freshly brewed, unsweetened tea, has no fat, calories, sodium or sugar. Green teas and herb teas are the best to drink if you wish to avoid a lot of caffeine or you could also choose from the wide variety of de-caffeinated versions of popular brands.

STORING TEA

Store tea in an airtight container, away from strong foods, and out of bright light. The subtle tastes of tea can easily be spoiled, and the dry leaves absorb moisture and other tastes and smells. Use a glass, china, or stainless steel container; other types can taint the tea.

Once opened, black tea, stored properly, will keep the longest—for up to a year. Green tea keeps less well—some for only a few months and certainly less than a year.

FRESHNESS MATTERS

Buy tea foil—wrapped or vacuum-packed if you intend to keep it long. Freshness does make a difference to the taste of tea. Tasters and blenders have several words in their tasting lexicon to describe tea that, though perfectly well made, has suffered from poor storage or shipping.

Chesty, for instance, means tea tainted by packaging materials. Mushy means tea that has not been stored in a dry place, and contains too much moisture. Baggy is tea tainted by hessian sacking. Gone off, as it suggests, is a term for bad tea kept too long.

THE PERFECT CUP OF TEA

Just slopping water onto a tea bag doesn't make the best tea—even though we've all done it. For your next cup, why not take your time, to try a few simple rules for perfect tea?

CHOOSE YOUR TEA

Choose tea to your taste, and to suit the occasion. Light teas such as Darjeeling and some Oolong teas are good in the afternoon. Green teas work well with or after meals. Black teas such as Assam, or Irish Breakfast, are excellent for strong morning tea.

BOIL YOUR WATER

Use water cold from the faucet, or even better, filtered water, especially if you live in a hard-water area. Only make tea when the water is boiling vigorously. Water that is overboiled or reboiled is flat, without the oxygen content that gives life to new-made tea.

USE A POT

Give tea space to brew properly, using a pot rather than a cup.

KEEP IT HOT

Warm the teapot with a little hot water—the aim is to keep the water as hot as possible while the tea is brewing; black tea in particular, only really brews well in the hottest water.

Keep the teapot clean by rinsing it regularly with hot water, or it can give a bitter taint to the next brew.

ADD THE TEA

Pour boiling water onto the tea. Use one teaspoon of tea per cup, and "one for the pot" if you like stronger tea. However, bear in mind that tea leaves vary in size and weight depending on the blend you are using, so experiment.

LET THE TEA BREW

Allow the tea to stand and brew, or infuse, for between three to five minutes —less for bags, more for loose tea.

This is the time it takes for the tea to release most of its characteristic flavors and stimulants, without becoming harsh or bitter.

After the tea is brewed, separate the leaves from the tea by pouring off the brewed tea into a second, warmed pot. Leave the tea and leaves together if you prefer, and enjoy the way the tea changes and becomes stronger as you finish the pot.

LOOSE TEA OR TEA BAGS?

Use bags for convenience and a quick brew, use loose tea when you want the best flavor. Loose tea floats freely and brews properly. All the best grades of tea are sold as loose tea.

GREEN, WHITE, AND OOLONG TEAS

Brew green teas differently from black. Don't use boiling water; slightly cooler water will give you the best results.

Many tea sellers recommend between 176°F (80°C) and 194°F (90°C), which means standing the boiled kettle for around five minutes before using the water. Or, add a dash of cold water to the leaves before pouring on the boiling water. Green teas will make multiple brews. For the first allow around a minute, depending on the tea. Some teas, such as the Japanese green tea Gyokuro, need as little as twenty seconds for the first brew. Drain the leaves, drink the tea, and brew again allowing slightly longer with each brew. Don't over-brew the tea, or it will quickly become bitter.

TEA PARAPHERNALIA

A whole range of infusers, filters and brewing mugs are available which make using loose-leaf tea convenient and mess free.

TEA TASTING

Most of the tea we know and recognize today is blended from original or single estate teas. Sometimes as many as 35 different teas will go to make just one of the popular brands.

Blends are created by tasters who assess and select teas, and blend them to long-followed recipes to create teas that are consistent, regardless of the weather conditions in the origin of the supply of tea.

A TASTER'S WORK

A taster may sample hundreds of teas in a single day. First they will assess the dry tea—judging its color, aroma, and the way it is twisted and made.

They look for tip, the downy silvering on tea leaves, which is a sign of the finest grades. The taster will then weigh samples, and brew each for a precise time—usually between five and six minutes. When the tea is brewed the liquid, or liquor, is poured into a tasting bowl. The leaves, or infusion, are then tipped onto the lid of the brewing mug.

The taster looks next at the infusion—looking for brightness and an even color. Only then does a taster sample the liquor itself—slurping the tea and sucking air over the tea and through the nose, like a wine taster, so that the tea is smelt, tasted and felt on the gums as it is swilled round the mouth, before it is spat out.

In many ways the tasting process is the same as that for wine. In fact, tea can vary in the same way, its quality depending on the season, the weather, and the skill of the maker.

BLACK TEAS

Most of the tea drunk in Europe and North America today is black tea. Most black tea originates from India, Sri Lanka, Kenya, and Indonesia.

Black teas have been allowed, in the language of tea, to ferment before being heated, dried, or fired. This fermentation lets the tea oxidize, taking on a deep coppery color, and giving black teas their distinctive rich flavor.

There are a huge variety of black teas. Rare China blacks, such as Russian Caravan and Prince of Wales, have the reputation as the most delicate. Black teas from India vary from the large-leafed, subtle teas of Darjeeling to the small-leafed, rich and malty teas of lowland Assam. Teas from Kenya, East Africa, and Sri Lanka are known for their bright coppery color.

English Breakfast is one of the most popular black teas.

It's designed to give a brisk start to the day, and to accompany food. It is traditionally a blend of small-leafed teas from Assam in India and Sri Lanka, and also Keemun teas from China. Today, many breakfast blends also include East African teas to give this blend of tea its characteristic coppery brightness.

The English Breakfast blend is, in fact, probably more Scottish than English. It was first blended by an Edinburgh tea merchant called Drysdale in the late 19th century, and sold there simply as Breakfast Tea.

It was well liked by Queen Victoria, a keen tea drinker who often spent time at the royal estate at Balmoral. The new Scottish tea was soon on sale in London where shops and merchants eventually changed its name, and sold it as English Breakfast Tea.

ENGLISH BREAKFAST

black tea

ORIGIN

Blended teas from India, Sri Lanka and East Africa

CHARACTER

- Robust, rich taste
- Bright coppery color
- Ideal accompaniment to breakfast
- Drink with milk, or lemon

45

RUSSIAN CARAVAN

black tea

Russian Caravan originated in 17th-century Russia. Merchants there sold two basic grades of tea.

The first, brick tea, was made from powdered, low-grade leaf, pressed into molds. Brick tea made the journey from China to Russia by sea. The second grade was high-quality black tea. At risk of spoiling on the voyage home, this tea was brought overland via Mongolia, on what must be one of history's longest, and most difficult trade routes.

The 11,000-mile journey by camel caravan took sixteen months. Supplies of tea were unpredictable and merchants blended teas from what was available to produce the high-quality robust flavour that the Russian aristocracy demanded. The opening of the Siberian railway in 1905 ended the caravan trade, but not the Russian love of strong-flavored tea which lives on in traditional forms of this blend.

TEA TIP
There is no single Russian Caravan blend. Some blends contain Lapsang Souchong, Indian teas and even Oolong teas from Taiwan

One-time British prime minister, Earl Grey, was presented with the first Earl Grey blend by a Chinese diplomat in the early 19th century.

It contained a still-secret blend of black teas, including the smoked tea, Lapsang Souchong. During the making of the tea bergamot citrus oil is added to flavor the tea.

The original Earl Grey formula is still held by Robert Jackson and Co, which was entrusted to a partner of the company by the original earl in 1830. Manufacturers today produce their own versions of Earl Grey.

Not all Earl Grey is the same. Lapsang Souchong, a smoky black tea, is included in most Earl Grey blends, but not in the Twining blend.

TEA TIP
Earl Grey is a flavored tea. Other flavored teas with strong aromas are: Jasmine, scented with jasmine flowers, and Rose Congou, scented with rose petals

EARL GREY

black tea

ORIGIN

Blended black tea from China flavored with bergamot citrus oil

CHARACTER

- Distinct mild, smoky tea with a citrus flavor

- Pale golden in color

- Refreshing tea for any time of day

- Drink black, with a little milk, or with lemon

49

DARJEELING

black tea

Darjeeling is grown in a hundred or so tea estates around the northeast Indian resort town of Darjeeling.

Many of the Darjeeling tea gardens are at altitudes of around 7,000 ft (2133 m), laid out on steep hillsides. This combination of altitude, soil, and climate gives Darjeeling tea its unique flavor.

The small-leafed tea is hand picked and processed using only rollers, and not the newer tearing, cutting and curling machinery. The Darjeeling picking season begins in March and lasts into October. The second flush Darjeelings, such as Puttabong, plucked between May and June, have the best reputation for delicacy and flavor.

When making this tea it is important not to over-brew it.

TEA TIP
Fans of Darjeeling should look out for the rare Darjeeling Green

ORIGIN

The foothills of the Himalayas, northeast India

CHARACTER

- Delicate muscatel taste
- Light golden color
- Traditionally an afternoon tea
- Drink black, or with a little milk

KEEMUN

black tea

Keemun is a Chinese black tea from the Qimen region of Anhui Province in Eastern China.

It was first introduced in 1875, probably in response to competition from Indian and Sri Lankan black teas.

Its flavor and character are produced by Qimen's high rainfall and misty mountain climate. It is picked from March through July; much of it is still done by hand.

Today Keemun is regarded as the classic China black tea, although this is a generic name given by the first merchants. In China itself Keemun is regarded as red tea. Keemun, with its tightly rolled leaf, is often used in Prince of Wales tea blends.

TEA TIP
The most prized Keemun teas are the leaf-bud and whole leaf grades picked in early spring

ORIGIN

Anhui Province,
Eastern China

CHARACTER

- A smooth-tasting tea with a toasted flavor and distinctive dark chocolaty aroma

- Rich burgundy color

LAPSANG SOUCHONG

black tea

Lapsang Souchong is black tea which has been smoked, giving it its unmistakable smoky flavor.

Legend has it that the first Lapsang Souchong was made when soldiers, camped in a tea factory, interrupted the drying process. When they had left, and needing to get the tea to market, the tea workers lit open pine wood fires to dry the tea—smoking it in the process.

Today Lapsang Souchong is still withered over fires of pine and cypress wood. The tea is then heated and rolled and left in barrels to ferment. It is fired and rolled again and then once more and hung in wood smoke. This involved process of rolling and smoking makes Lapsang Souchong tea a uniquely large-leafed tea.

YUNNAN

black tea

The majority of black China tea comes from Yunnan. It is high-grown, mountain tea produced from an ancient strain of tea variety, which is also used for Pu'er medicinal tea.

The Yunnan tea bush has broad, soft leaves and fat shoots. Yunnan tea is known as big leaf, and produces a full-bodied, brisk-flavored tea. In other regions of China, tea strains with narrow, thin leaves are more typical.

The tea plant is thought to have originated in Yunnan, and the mountain soils, mists, and sub-tropical climate combine for perfect tea-growing conditions. Many wild tea trees still grow in the province— the oldest known is thought to be over a 1,000 years old and is 108 ft (33m) tall.

TEA TIP
Yunnan is also the source of the rare modern-day brick and compressed China teas

ORIGIN

Yunnan Province, southwest China

CHARACTER

- Mellow malt, peppery flavor
- Bright golden color
- Drink any time
- Drink black or with a little milk

ASSAM

black tea

ORIGIN

The flood plains of
the Assam valley,
northeast India

CHARACTER

- Rich, strong and
  malty flavor

- Deep amber color

- Traditionally a morning or
  breakfast tea

- Drink with a little milk

Assam tea is grown on more than 600 tea estates on the sweeping flood plains of the Brahmaputra River in the Assam Valley, northeast of India.

The rich soil, rain and humidity make ideal tea-growing conditions, and Assam is the biggest tea-producing region of India. Assam teas are often used in blends to give a characteristic rich, malty flavor.

Most Assam tea is known as rain tea, as it is produced between August and mid October during the monsoon season. Plantations shaded by large trees often have the fastest growing bushes.

The finest Assam tea is the second flush picking, known for the fine silvery hair —or tip—on the leaf which helps distinguish the flavor and liquor of Assam tea from all others. The picking season in Assam runs from late March to December.

TEA TIP
Try Assam Green, a rare and unusual green tea that tastes almost sweet

GREEN TEAS

Green teas—lighter, and more subtle in flavor than black teas—are the world's oldest varieties. The Chinese tea, Green Gunpowder, may be the oldest tea, at possibly over 5,000 years old. Today in China, Japan and across the east, most of the tea drunk is green.

Unlike black tea, green teas are not withered or fermented after they are picked. Instead, after the tea is plucked, the green leaf is steamed (though not always) which kills and curls the leaf. The tea is then

generally fired until it is crisp. Green tea is among the least processed of all teas; it has the reputation as the most healthy, and has been connected with reducing the risks of heart disease, strokes, cancers and dementia.

There are at least 1,000 varieties of green tea, and many variations in green tea manufacture.

Often Chinese farmers produce their own tea, and use their own special individual processes.

The leaves of many green teas will happily make more than one brew at each sitting.

TEA TIP
Green tea will begin to deteriorate within six months of manufacture, and special care is needed in storing. It should be kept in an airtight container in a cool place away from sunlight

LUNG CHING

green tea

Lung Ching translates as Dragon Well.

It is made from tea bush buds, and each pound contains around 25,000 hand-picked buds. The tea is not rolled, but as soon after it is picked as possible it is fired, often by hand in open pans.

Zhejiang Province is renowned for its green teas, but other provinces of China also produce green tea for export—including Monkey King tea from Anhui Province, where black Keemun tea is produced.

Some of the finest Chinese green teas are still rolled and fired by hand—in fact some cannot be produced any other way. Chun Mee, also from Anhui Province, meaning literally "precious eyebrows," requires leaves to be rolled by hand, to the correct shape, at the right temperature for the correct length of time.

ORIGIN

Zhejiang Province, China

CHARACTER

- Fresh, aromatic flavor, slightly sweet

- Clear jade color

- Considered a cooling tea; often served in hot weather

- Drink without milk

63

GREEN GUNPOWDER

green tea

ORIGIN

Zhejiang Province, China

CHARACTER

Fragrant, lingering taste •

Rich green color •

Can be served with meals •

Green gunpowder is probably one of the world's oldest kinds of tea.

Seventeenth-century tea merchants dubbed the tea gunpowder because of its pellet-like appearance. The Chinese call it pearl tea.

Green gunpowder is a whole-leaf tea, painstakingly fired and rolled by hand. Several firings are used to dry the tea, and prevent it fermenting. At each stage the tea is rolled and allowed to cool. By the end of the manufacturing process each bud is a small, rolled, green pellet.

As gunpowder tea is brewed, its individual buds unfurl and release their flavor.

SENCHA

green tea

Sencha is Japan's most popular and widely drunk green tea.

The dark green, flat, needle-like leaves give a pale yellow tea with a delicate flavor. The name Sencha is an old reference to its way of manufacture, and literally means roasted tea. Today's Sencha teas are steamed before they are dried with hot air, processed and fired.

Japan, though one of the oldest tea-growing countries in the world, exports only a tiny percentage of its production and Sencha teas are often hard to find. The Sencha teas with the best reputation are sin-cha, or early season teas, picked before the end of May from the tea bushes' new growth.

TEA TIP
In Japan, Sencha is a good, everyday tea. For special occasions the tea to choose is Gyokuro, Precious Dew

ORIGIN

Japan

CHARACTER

- Delicate grassy taste, almost sweet

- Pale yellow color

- Refreshing tea that goes well with light meals

OOLONG TEAS

Oolong teas are semi-green. They have a flowery, peach aroma, and do not need milk, sugar, or lemon.

The leaves are only partly fermented when the tea is manufactured. Gently agitated by hand, the leaves turn a rich red at the edge, before they are dried or fired over charcoal. Taiwan and China both produce Oolong teas.

Those from Taiwan go by the name of Formosa Oolongs, and are often fermented a little longer than the lighter China Oolongs. The China Oolongs are in turn more heavily roasted than those from Taiwan. The best China Oolongs originate in Fujian and Guangdong Provinces.

Tea made with Oolong is anything from a deep red to pale cherry in color. For instance, Se Zhong is a strong, rich Oolong tea, while Shu Xian, or Water Fairy, is a light, subtle tea.

THE BEST OOLONG TEAS

The best Oolong teas, like many Chinese green teas, are still produced by individual farmers. These teas are unique, expensive, do not keep long, and are not often exported. Many of them fall into the category of sacred garden teas which, during Imperial times were produced only for the Emperor and the court, and even today are still very hard to come by.

Listed in the following pages are some of the better-known Oolongs available.

TEA TIP
Oolong means black dragon, after the long, twisted black leaf which characterizes Oolong tea

TI KWAN YIN

oolong tea

Ti kwan yin, or Iron Goddess of Mercy tea, is a rare Oolong tea.

Its large, dark, crinkly leaves are rolled lengthways, by hand, and unfurl as the tea is brewed.

According to legend, the goddess of mercy appeared in a dream to a farmer in Fujian Province. She told him of a treasure hidden behind the temple dedicated to her. When the farmer looked he found a tiny tea bush. From this bush comes the fragrant tea named after the goddess.

ORIGIN

Fujian Province, China

CHARACTER

- Subtle but distinctive flavor

- Pale golden color

- Drink with meals, or on its own

- Don't add milk or sugar. Oolong teas can be an acquired taste if you are used to black tea drunk the English way

POUCHONG

oolong tea

ORIGIN

Taiwan and also Fujian
Province, China

CHARACTER

- Distinct, fresh almost
sweet taste

- Light golden color

- Drink black, without milk
or sugar

Pouchong is the least processed of Oolong teas. Its large, long, lightly fermented leaves are almost like a green tea.

Originally the leaves of this tea were wrapped in paper during the light fermentation process. Now the leaves are withered in the sun for an hour or so, and allowed to cool in the shade. The leaves are tossed and lightly agitated to ferment them before being roasted and rolled.

Pouchong originates from the Pinlin region near Taipei, Taiwan. Settlers from Fujian in China originally brought the Oolong technique to the island in the 1850s. Today Pouchong from Taiwan has the best reputation of all Oolong teas, though many Pouchong Oolongs are also produced in China.

TEA TIP
Light Pouchong teas are often used as the base for scented teas, with rose petals or jasmine flowers added during the processing to produce fragrant flowery teas

CHINA WHITE TEAS

White teas are among the world's rarest. The secret is in the time and the way in which they are picked.

Traditionally, white tea is picked only in the first weeks of spring and before dawn, when the tender new buds have yet to open. It is neither fermented nor fired, but air dried. Only particular strains of the China bush are used, and even then only certain bushes and parts of a tea garden might be picked.

White tea originates from Fujian Province in China. This is still the center of white tea production, though Sri Lanka now also produces white teas.

As white tea is so slightly processed it contains more antioxidants (similar to those found in many fruits and vegetables) than any other tea. These antioxidants have been linked to reducing cholesterol and reducing the risk of heart disease. Western cosmetic firms are also beginning to use white teas for skin preparations.

White tea gets it name from the fine down (like the hair on a peach) that covers the new leaves and gives them their characteristic fine, silver-white color.

TEA TIP

White teas are brewed in the same way as green tea, with water that is well below boiling. The leaves will make multiple brews, but each brew should be left for one to three minutes, and quickly poured from the leaves to prevent bitterness

WHITE PEKEO

china white

White Pekeo tea is hardly processed, but is made from only carefully selected, unopened spring buds picked before dawn.

The leaves are not rolled or fermented, but withered and dried using a combination of sunshine and shade.

Pekeo (said "peck-oh") is a Chinese word that is also used in the general grading of tea. It means hair or down, and the name White Pekeo comes from this tea's silvered, downy look.

TEA TIP

White Peony, or Pai Mu Tan, is another white tea sometimes available outside China.

It is made from the smallest buds, which are steamed before they are dried. As the buds are steamed they open like blossoms, giving the tea its name

ORIGIN

Fujian Province, China

CHARACTER

- Mellow taste with a hint of sweetness

- Pale, clear color

SILVER NEEDLE

china white

ORIGIN

Fujian Province, China

CHARACTER

- Clean, mellow taste
- Fresh honey-sweet fragrance
- Pale yellow brew
- Do not add sugar or milk

Silver Needle tea is grown in the high mountains of Fujian Province.

The tea is made only from buds picked in the first few weeks of spring, before dawn when the leaves are still heavy with dew. These closed, silvered, downy buds are gently rolled and dried to give the long, characteristically silver needle appearance.

This tea is painstakingly made by hand to very high standards. For instance, silver needle tea is not picked when it rains, and buds that are damaged or too old are rejected.

TEA TIP
White teas are delicately flavored—and expensive. Brew them carefully, using filtered water. In the past, wealthy Chinese tea drinkers would have water brought in from mountain springs hundreds of miles away

HERBAL TEAS AND TISANES

Tea itself was first used as a herbal tea and remedy. It was thought of as just one of many herbs that could be used to treat illness and stimulate the body and mind.

Today, herbal teas and tisanes made from the flowers, roots, leaves, berries, and seeds of edible plants, are still popular. Although many herbal teas are not technically tea, because they contain no leaves from the tea plant *camellia sinensis*, they are easily prepared and can be enjoyed in much the same way as tea. Many also have added health benefits and most are caffeine free. The most popular true tisanes are chamomile, peppermint, and nettle; these make fine iced teas, as does Rooibos tea from South Africa.

Fruit and spiced teas are also widely available. These teas, for instance apple or blackcurrent, often consist of traditional tea blended with fruit, or flavored with fruit juice or zest. Other fruit teas are flavored with spices such as cinnamon or nutmeg.

Pure fruit teas contain no real tea, but are blended from fruits and herbs, usually containing rose hip and hibiscus.

TEA TIP
While you can buy most herbal teas as off-the-shelf bags, you can brew herbal teas using your own homegrown herbs. Chop herbs and brew in the same way as tea; experiment to get a strength you prefer. You can also dry herbs to store them. Bear in mind that some plants are poisonous, and only use plants that you are confident you know and recognize

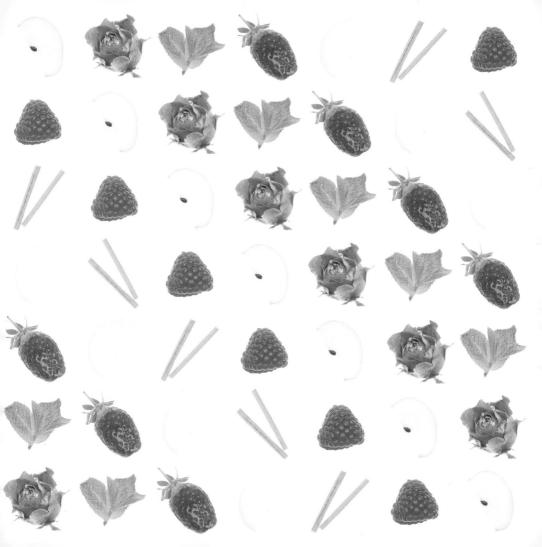

ROOIBOS

herbal tea

Rooibos, or red bush, tea is made from the fine needle leaves of a South African plant, aspalathus linearis.

Its reputation is as a healthy, tasty, and aromatic alternative to tea. It is rich in potassium and sodium, and contains iron, calcium, copper, zinc, magnesium, fluoride, and manganese.

Originally a wild plant, native of the Western Cape region of South Africa, Rooibos was first used for tea at the end of the 19th century. The plants were cut and then bruised with hammers, allowing the leaves to ferment in much the same way as tea.

Today Rooibos is farmed. New plants are grown for each crop. The seeds are sown in spring, and harvested eighteen months later. The plants are cut, and bound in bundles, rolled and fermented—taking on their characteristically deep red color.

PROPERTIES

Caffeine free, reputed to calm and soothe

FLAVOR

- Fruity and sweet tasting
- Deep red and orange colors

PU'ER

h e r b a l   t e a

ORIGIN

Large leaf black tea from
Pu'er, Yunnan Province,
southwest China.
It is reputed to be a
health drink, particularly
aiding digestion

CHARACTER

Unusual earthy taste ●

Musty aroma ●

Drink after rich meals ●

*Pu'er is tea that has been fermented twice—
the second time by bacteria which gives the
tea its dark, earthy character. Pu'er is
named after the town where this tea was
first collected and traded.*

Pu'er comes in many forms, including as
loose tea, but most often as compressed
tea, made into bricks and cakes. This
form of compressed tea (though not
necessarily Pu'er) is still favored in some
regions of China and Tibet, and it is this
original form of tea that was once used
as currency.

Unlike any other tea, Pu'er improves
with age. Even at ten years old the tea is
still called young. At this age it still has
an astringent green tea flavour. As Pu'er
teas become older, and rarer, the tea
takes on subtle and more complex flavors
even after thirty years.

In China Pu'er is valued for its medicinal
qualities, and as an aid to digestion. Pu'er
contains the same kinds of antioxidants
as green tea, often associated with health
benefits such as lowered cholesterol.

CHAMOMILE

herbal tea

Chamomile is one of the most popular of herbal teas, with a long history of use in folk medicine.

In medieval Germany, chamomile was recommended for relieving indigestion. The herb was used in ancient Egypt to treat malaria.

There are three kinds of chamomile, but only the Roman and German types bear the aromatic flowers from which tea can be made.

Most tea merchants will sell chamomile teas, but it is also possible to grow the herb for yourself. Chamomile is perennial, and once sown will appear year after year. Sow from seed in spring, in full sun, in light, well-drained soil. Pick and dry flowers for tea-making once they are fully opened.

TEA TIP
Other teas to try for relaxation are lemon balm and peppermint

PROPERTIES

Chamomile is reputed to calm, helping relieve anxiety and stress, and soothe digestion. It also helps relaxation.

FLAVOUR

- Bright, clear, golden tea
- Soft, musty aroma with apple taste

MINT TEA

h e r b a l   t e a

PROPERTIES

Mint, peppermint in particular,
is believed to refresh, calm
and aid digestion

FLAVOR

Strongly aromatic ●

Mint tea can be bought as a dried herbal tea, or tisane, and makes a pleasant after-meal drink, with a reputation for helping digestion.

But there is another mint tea, a speciality of Morocco, which is served steaming in a small glass and thick with sugar. Mint tea made the Moroccan way, on a base of green tea, also makes good iced tea.

Make mint tea with one teaspoon of green tea per cup, with two teaspoons of sugar, and a bunch of fresh mint. Brew the tea, sugar and mint together in the pot. As with all green teas don't brew it too hot (around 194°F/90°C) or too long, as this will turn it bitter. When mint is scarce Moroccan tea drinkers also use sage, basil, or marjoram.

TEA TIP
There are two main kinds of mint, both with distinct flavors: spearmint and peppermint. Spearmint has a warm aromatic taste. Peppermint has a clean, sharp menthol taste

FRUIT TEA

Many fruit teas—in fact tisanes, because they have no real tea in them—were originally created as healthy, pleasant drinks for children.

Rose hip tea is the original fruit tisane, traditionally a blend of rose hips and hibiscus. This tea has a mildly tart, lemony taste and is particularly rich in vitamin C. It is also caffeine free.

The rose hip and hibiscus blend is used as the base for many fruit tisanes. The range available is huge; anything from orange to ginger to raspberry.

TEA TIP
Fruit tisanes are those which contain no true tea.
Fruit tea is flavored tea

PROPERTIES

Fruit teas are pleasant brews rich in vitamin C

FLAVOR

- Full, fruity aromas, with tangy, sweet flavors.

- Often made on a base of hibiscus flowers and rose hips

ICED TEA

Around eighty per cent of the tea drunk in America is iced tea. It was invented during a heatwave at the 1904 St Louis World Trade Fair.

Plantation owner Richard Blechynden had planned to attract visitors, and sales, by giving away free samples of his tea. But, because of the heat, no one was interested, until in a moment of inspiration he decided to serve the tea poured into glasses packed with ice.

INGREDIENTS

Iced tea works best made with Ceylon or China Keemun. Use more tea than you would normally use to counteract the ice; about twice as much, depending on your taste. Fruit tea also works well iced, as does mint tea.

MAKING ICED TEA

How to make perfect iced tea.

- *Keemun or Ceylon black tea*
- *Ice*
- *Pitcher*
- *Long glasses*
- *Fresh lemon or mint*

METHOD

Brew the tea, for between three and five minutes, using double the usual amount of tea.

Fill a pitcher two thirds full with ice—an amount equal to the double-strength tea you have brewed.

The moment the tea is brewed, pour it onto the ice, using a strainer if necessary.

By pouring the tea straight onto the ice the sudden cooling preserves the flavor of the tea, and prevents the cloudiness that often develops in black tea as it is cooled.

Garnish with mint or lemon. Make green iced tea in the same way, but make sure not to overbrew the green tea as it quickly becomes bitter.

CHAI

Chai is the national drink of India. Chai means tea in Hindi, and comes from the Cantonese Chaa. Chai is hot, spiced milk tea. It is sold everywhere and made at home to treasured family recipes to welcome guests and visitors. It is even becoming popular in America, sometimes being sold as tea latte.

INGREDIENTS

Chai is generally made from a base of rich black tea, heavy milk, a combination of spices and sugar, molasses, honey or condensed milk. In traditional Indian recipes, the spices vary from region to region but the most common are cardamom, cinnamon, ginger, cloves, and pepper. You can also use coriander, dark unsweetened chocolate, licorice root (though use sparingly), vanilla, and nutmeg.

Assam or Keemun teas, with their robust flavors, work well in Chai. But lighter teas also work with the right spices. For instance, light Darjeeling tea can combine well for a simple Chai made with cardamom.

To make Chai, start by brewing the spices and sugar for about six minutes. Only add the tea leaves at this stage if you like strong tea. Add milk, and bring almost to the boil. Take off the heat, add the tea and let the mixture brew for three to five minutes. Strain and serve.

Making Chai

These are two basic Chai recipes. Adjust them to your taste and experiment to make your own personal Chai.

Chai—Serves 2

2 whole cloves
1 cardamom pod
¹/₂ cinnamon stick, broken into pieces
1¹/₂ cups water
¹/₈ teaspoon ground ginger
pinch of freshly ground black pepper
¹/₄ of a cup milk
1 tablespoon sugar
1 tablespoon black tea

Method

• Crush the cloves, cardamom pods, and cinnamon.

• Place in a pan and add the water, ginger and pepper and bring to the boil.

• Remove from the heat, and allow to brew for five minutes.

• Add the milk and sugar, and boil once more.

• Remove from the heat, add the tea, cover, and brew for three minutes.

• Strain and serve in warmed glasses.

Green Chai—Serves 2

2¹/₄ cups water
2 cardamom pods, whole, split
³/₄ cup milk
6 teaspoons sugar
2 teaspoons green tea or Darjeeling

Method

• Bring the water and milk almost to a boil.

• Add the cardamom and brew for three minutes.

• Add tea. Stir lightly.

• Brew for two minutes more.

• Strain and serve in warm glasses.

TEA CEREMONIES

Tea is central to the welcome and entertainment of guests in cultures the world over. Many countries have very formal etiquette and even ceremonies for the serving of tea.

The taste and types of modern-day tea ceremonies vary hugely, as does the tea. In Malaysia, the taking of tea is practically a national pastime but not every nation would approve of the tea, brewed for several hours in a metal pot.

In Mali, West Africa, tea drinkers have a formal daily gathering where people meet in what are known as grins for the ceremony of the three teas. The first cup is brewed strong, like life. The second is sweet, like love. The third is bitter, like death.

While few see the British idea of afternoon tea as a ceremony, it began very like one, as a very formal occasion with extremely strict rules. For instance, in 18th-century Britain you could not refuse a cup of tea, and if a guest to tea did not know to balance their spoon on the rim of their cup, they would be served cup after cup until they burst.

THE JAPANESE TEA CEREMONY

Tea was probably introduced to Japan from China in the 8th century, and the way it is drunk today, and the character of the Japanese tea ceremony, partly dates from that time. Tea is still often regarded with reverence; its name "o-cha" means honorable tea.

The Japanese tea ceremony, or "chanoyu," traditionally takes place in a wooden or bamboo tea house set on its own. No more than five guests take part, and around the tea house there is a garden of green plants, a rock garden, and a stream. A path winds its way through the garden. The tea house contains a low table and is plainly decorated.

The chanoyu is all about appreciating and focusing on simple, beautiful things. Guests are greeted in the garden, and enter the tea house. At various stages in the ceremony they will admire the beauty of the room and its contents. The host—the tea master—then brings in the tea utensils, arranges them with care and begins to make tea. The powdered green tea leaves are placed in the tea bowl and hot, but not boiling, water is poured over them. The tea is then whisked as it was in 8th century China. When it is ready it is passed to each guest in turn. As the guests take the bowl from where it is placed in front of them, they turn it so they do not drink from the side that faced them. Turning the bowl means that, though the side you were given was the best, you are not good enough to drink from it.

Japan also has a more relaxed form of the tea ceremony, known as "sencha." Most Japanese will take part. Those who don't have tea houses belong to a tea club which meets for the tea ceremony.

CHINESE TEA CEREMONY

The Chinese tea ceremony is about the taste and smell of tea. The ceremony is not formal, but it is thought special. It is a time to relax and enjoy tea in company.

The tea ceremony varies across China, but in most areas the tea is made in small clay teapots. This preparation of tea ("Cha Dao") is regarded as an art form.

The pot is rinsed in boiling water, and then the tea leaves added with a bamboo scoop or chopsticks. The water for the tea is important. It must be hot, but not too hot to spoil the taste of the green tea.

The tea is brewed for less than a minute. The cups are arranged in a circle. Then the tea is poured in one movement. Each cup is filled only halfway—the rest of the cup is believed to be filled by friendship.

RUSSIAN TEA CEREMONY

Tea is a Russian passion. The focus of tea making is the "samovar," a tea kettle first used in the distinctive tea-drinking style of the prerevolutionary Russian aristocracy. It is often placed at the center of the dinner table when the meal is finished.

Samovars consist of a large, water-heating urn with one, and sometimes, two teapots which sit on top to keep warm. The middle pot will usually hold the strong black tea favored by Russians, and the top pot herbal or mint tea. Teas can be

mixed or diluted, and each drinker can have the tea they like. Russian tea is drunk black, sometimes with lemon or sugar, and even fruit jelly (often placed on the tongue) is used to sweeten it.

Samovars are often decorated with scenes from folk tales, or sometimes fit together to look like a person or an animal. The tea is often drunk from small wire-handled glasses or "podstakanniki."

KOREAN TEA CEREMONY

In Korea, the tea ceremony is used by Buddhist monks to help meditation and concentration. Called "Panyaro" or the dew of wisdom, the ceremony is the brewing, serving and drinking of green Oolong tea.

The ceremony—similar in many ways to those of China and Japan—uses pure spring water. Traditionally it is not used boiling, but hot, to get the best flavour from the tea. A traditional tea set, of five cups with wooden saucers, a teapot, two bowls, and a small stand is used, and three successive brews are made.

The Panyaro is a less formal occasion than its Japanese counterpart but many families will hold a tea ceremony at times of celebration.

TEAWARE

When tea first arrived in Europe it was so new and strange that no one had anything appropriate to drink it from, let alone items to store or make it in.

All teaware was imported and deemed as important as the tea itself. Wealthy women in 18th-century Boston would carry their tea bowls with them when they visited neighbors.

As the trade in tea grew so did the demand for all manner of tea paraphernalia; from sugar dishes to tea tongs, to tea spoons, kettles, and low tables or tea tables, convenient for serving tea. In fact, many British craftsmen feared for their jobs because of the level of imports. One protest petition, started by the London Joiners' company at the end of the 17th century, reveals that 6,582 tea tables had been imported over a four-year period.

TEA CADDIES

The earliest tea caddies, were the fine porcelain canisters imported from China. Used to hold loose tea, their lids would often double as measures. Before long, caddies began to take the form of small caskets, complete with locks. Tea was so expensive that only the mistress of the house would have access to tea and she would wear the caddy key on a chain around her waist.

TEAPOTS

The first teapots in Europe arrived on the same East Indiamen boats as the tea. At first they were the small, unglazed, red stoneware pots, adapted from water ewers, that were favored by the Chinese themselves. Often these were made in Yixing in Jiangsu Province—still the center of Chinese teapot making today.

Glazed porcelain teapots like those used in the Chinese Imperial court followed. At the time no one in Europe could even make porcelain and such pots, with their delicate white glaze and images of flowers, birds and figures were a great luxury. Even if they broke, teapots were often not thrown away but repaired with rivets or with replacement metal spouts.

Novelty and the teapot have long been associated. Even the first unglazed, red clay teapots were often made in fanciful shapes. In Britain, from about 1760, teapots began to appear made in the shape of cauliflowers, pineapples, and pears. Design remains important for teapots—from the bold art deco designs of Clarice Cliff to the modern glass infusers, and the Lyons teapot with two spouts.

MILK FIRST, OR TEA FIRST?

The first fine Chinese porcelain tea bowls would often crack when hot or boiling tea was poured into them. To prevent this, many people put milk in first—perhaps the origin of the milk first tradition. It wasn't until around 1800 that the problem was solved. British potters learnt to make a tough, fine porcelain that contained ground cattle bones; they called it bone china.

GROW YOUR OWN TEA

Though the tea plant is a native of Asia, it can grow surprisingly well in domestic gardens. It is one of the camellia family, and its dark evergreen leaves make it a pleasant all-year plant for pots, patios, and borders. It lends itself to clipping and shaping and can be very long lived; the oldest is reputed to be more than a 1,000 years old. Also camellias do not need a lot of attention.

WHICH TEA?

There are four varieties of *camellia sinensis*. The China variety is the best to grow domestically, as this is the most hardy and will put up with more varied climates. It is also the smallest growing of the tea varieties, a bush rather than a tree, some of which will grow to over 100 ft (30 m).

WHERE TO PLANT

Tea, like most camellias, likes partial or dappled shade as the plants tend to scald in hot sun. Tea in Assam, India, is often grown under a shady tree canopy for this very reason.

Choose a position with shade, sheltered from cold winds. Also shade from early morning sun, as this is the most likely time for damage to buds and flowers.

Soil

Tea likes moist but well-drained and acid soil (between pH 5 and 6.5). Plants don't like to be planted too deep; the top of their root ball should be level with the firmed surface of the soil. Improve the soil pH if necessary with leaf mold or cow manure.

Caring for your tea bush

Tea doesn't need a great deal of attention, but it does need water in dry weather.

Tea needs a cool winter, and will tolerate moderate frosts. In heavy frosts, plants will need protecting. To keep your tea plant small and to encourage flowers it can be pruned back to just above the old wood. Prune in spring after the plant has flowered.

THE TEA GARDEN

The concept of a Japanese tea garden is more than a thousand years old. In essence it is about creating a quiet, reflective space.

The designs for traditional tea gardens have simplicity and order, and contain the essential elements of water, green plants, stone, and bridges.

With only a limited budget it is possible to recreate the special calm of a Japanese tea garden yourself, even in small spaces.

TEA HOUSE

Traditionally tea houses are simple but elegant structures from which the garden can be quietly contemplated. Create your own tea house using a pergola, trained with plants.

PATH

A path can be created with stepping stones. It should draw the eye, winding through the garden, creating perspective.

WATER

Tea gardens have streams which are symbolic of nature. It is possible to create streams with pumps and channels, and even to include bridges. But a simple pool, if only a small one, can also provide interest and beauty.

PLANTS

The emphasis in a tea garden is on foliage and texture, not flowers. Grow shrubs that can be trained or shaped. Plant modest hedges. Use sculptural, evergreen plants, and scented, evergreen herbs. Use moss and ground-covering plants.

STONE

Use gravel to create a smooth, simple landscape that frames and joins the elements of the garden. Place large stones as features.

READING THE LEAVES

Some people believe that the way tea leaves fall in a person's cup can reveal their future. Whether or not you believe it, reading the leaves can be an entertaining way to share tea with friends.

Use loose leaf tea, and no strainer, so that leaves pour with the tea from the pot. Drink the tea, and leave a little at the bottom of the cup. Swill the dregs round the cup, three times clockwise, and three times back. Pour the liquid away, and place the cup in front of you. You are now ready to read the leaves.

WHAT TO LOOK FOR

In reading leaves, or tassology as it's often known, the key is to look for pictures and symbols formed by the leaves. A key, for instance, indicates secrets. A swarm of bees suggests a gathering or party is coming. A lake suggests calm.

Different areas of the cup represent aspects of your life, those nearest the rim are current, or soon-to-happen events.

Pictures and symbols nearest the center of the cup represent your emotional life.

Read the cup clockwise from the handle. The first half of the cup usually concerns the family. The second arc of the cup refers to events outside the family.

Turn the page to find a dictionary of symbols and their meanings.

SECRETS OF THE LEAVES

A brief guide to the symbols in your cup:

Anchor a problem will be answered
Apple good health and happiness
Arrow (down) bad luck
Arrow (up) good luck
Axe you will be rid of burdens
Bird good luck will arrive
Bone be cautious
Bridge a time for change and travel
Castle expect a legacy
Chicken change is on the way
Clouds worry
Eagle courage
Egg success is likely
Face change is likely
Fire foolishness will destroy something
Hat visitor
Heart love
Key secrets
Lake peace

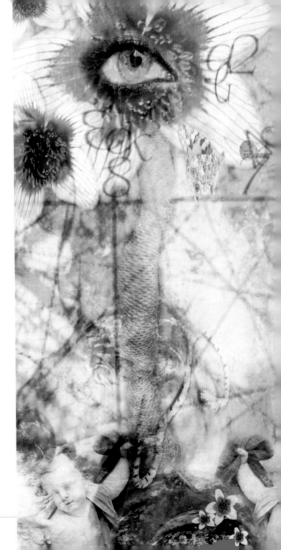

Loop avoid acting on impulse
Monkey stop, think
Palm tree creativity
Seahorse self-indulgence is necessary
Shark trouble
Swarm of bees a gathering is close
Sword move quickly
Tower events will take an
unexpected turn
Triangle child
Vase a friend is in need of advice
or consolation
Volcano things are about to come to
a head
Web an omen
Wheel a sign of progress
Windmill a personal venture
will succeed
Wings an interesting message is on
its way
Yacht money worries will lessen

MAKING MORE OF TEA

**Tea is versatile and subtle.
Here are some simple ideas
for exotically flavored teas.**

ORCHARD TEA

A refreshing apple tea.

YOU WILL NEED

- 1 part Darjeeling tea
- 1 part apple juice
- 1 apple

METHOD

Brew the Darjeeling for three
to five minutes, and strain. Add the
apple juice and heat in a pan, but
do not boil.

SERVE

Serve hot in cups, with apple slices.

SUMMER TEA

Perfect for a hot day in the garden.

YOU WILL NEED

- 2 cups water
- 5 teaspoons Assam tea
- 2 oz (57 g) sugar
- 1 ½ cup orange juice
- 2 oz (57 g) strawberries

METHOD

Boil the water and pour over the tea. Brew for three to five minutes and then strain. Add the sugar and orange juice and leave to cool in the fridge.

SERVE

In tall glasses with ice, lemon and strawberries. Add brandy or rum if you wish.

APRICOT SAMOVAR

A special but quickly made tea with a traditional Russian flavour.

YOU WILL NEED

1 cup strong black tea
1 tablespoon apricot jelly, or other favorite jelly
dark sugar
cream

METHOD

Brew the tea, and add the fruit jelly and sugar. Stir well, and add cream if you wish.

SERVE

The Russian way is to put the jam on the tongue, and drink the tea black. This way you can taste the bitter tea and sweet jelly together.

Halakahiki tea

A perfect fruit tea for friends.

You will need

1 pint (570 ml) boiling water
1/2 cup loose tea
2 tablespoons mint leaves
1 pint (570 ml) cold water
1/2 lemon juice
1/2 cup sugar
1/2 cup pineapple juice
fresh pineapple

Method

Place the mint and tea in a pan,
and pour on boiling water. Cover
and allow to brew for five minutes.
Strain in jug containing the cold
water. Add lemon juice, pineapple
juice, and sugar.

Serve

Pour into glasses over ice. Garnish
with mint and pineapple pieces.

123

BLACK RUSSIAN TEA

A perfect warming cocktail of tea and wine.

YOU WILL NEED

1 ½ pints (284 ml) good black tea
4 tablespoons lemon juice
4 tablespoons sugar
4 cloves
1 pint (570 ml) red wine
1 lemon, sliced
stick of cinnamon

METHOD

Heat all the ingredients, except the lemon, in a pan.

SERVE

Strain into tall glasses and garnish with the lemon.

Planters' tea

A stiff drink to sit back and relax with.

You will need

    2 pints (1141 ml) strong black tea
    1 pint (570 ml) dark rum
    $\frac{1}{2}$ pint (284 ml) orange juice
    $\frac{1}{4}$ pint (142 ml) lemon juice
    soft brown sugar
    sliced orange and lemon

Method

Heat the tea, the rum, orange, and lemon juice in a pan, but do not boil.

Serve

Add sugar to taste and garnish with orange and lemon.

Royal Bengal tea

A long, royal drink for one.

You will need

- 1 teaspoon lemon juice
- 2 dashes angostura bitters
- $\frac{1}{2}$ teaspoon dark sugar
- 1 measure of cognac
- 1 cup cold, strong tea

Method

Mix the lemon, sugar, cognac, and bitters in the bottom of a tall glass.

Serve

Fill with ice and pour over the tea. Garnish with lemon and mint.

EVENING MIST

Just the tea to share on a misty
Scottish evening.

YOU WILL NEED

1 cup good black tea
1 measure whisky
3 teaspoons honey
cream (optional)

METHOD

Heat the tea, whisky, and honey
together in a pan, but do not boil.

SERVE

With a topping of cream if desired.

THE WORLD DRINK

The world produces nearly three million tonnes of tea every year; it seems we can't get quite enough.

From green, black, herbal, and mint, from the rare mountain teas of China, collected only at dawn, to pyramid tea bags—tea is as versatile and as different as the people who drink it. New ways to enjoy tea are constantly being invented—from the American iced tea, to ready-brewed canned Oolong tea, and even Taiwanese bubble tea, made with tapioca.

But while tea is ever popular the way we buy it could be about to undergo a revolution—internet shopping. The internet makes speciality, single estate teas ever easier to find. We can all still enjoy our favorite tea bag brand, but at the same time track down rare and unusual teas from named estates in all corners of the world.

But even if our tea tastes change, one thing about tea stays the same—it is recognized the world over as an opportunity to relax, and to share time and talk with friends.